LACROSSE

WHO DOES WHAT?

BY RYAN NAGELHOUT

 Gareth Stevens
PUBLISHING

Please visit our website, www.garethstevens.com. For a free color catalog of all our high-quality books, call toll free 1-800-542-2595 or fax 1-877-542-2596.

Cataloging-in-Publication Data

Names: Nagelhout, Ryan.
Title: Lacrosse: who does what? / Ryan Nagelhout.
Description: New York : Gareth Stevens Publishing, 2018. | Series: Sports: what's your position? | Includes index.
Identifiers: ISBN 9781538204337 (pbk.) | ISBN 9781538204115 (library bound) | ISBN 9781538204344 (6 pack)
Subjects: LCSH: Lacrosse–Juvenile literature.
Classification: LCC GV989.14 N34 2018 | DDC 796.36'2–dc23

First Edition

Published in 2018 by
Gareth Stevens Publishing
111 East 14th Street, Suite 349
New York, NY 10003

Copyright © 2018 Gareth Stevens Publishing

Designer: Sarah Liddell
Editor: Ryan Nagelhout

Photo credits: Cover, pp. 1, 5, 9, 25, 27 James A. Boardman/Shutterstock.com; jersey texture used throughout Al Sermeno Photography/Shutterstock.com; chalkboard texture used throughout Maridav/Shutterstock.com; pp. 7, 15, 19 (grass) ANURAK PONGPATIMET/Shutterstock.com; pp. 8, 18, 28 Larry St. Pierre/Shutterstock.com; p. 11 Mike Broglio/Shutterstock.com; p. 13 Justin Edmonds/Stringer/Getty Images Sport/Getty Images; p. 14 Icon Sports Wire/Contributor/Icon Sportswire/Getty Images; p. 17 Doug Pensinger/Staff/Getty Images Sport/Getty Images; pp. 21, 23 The Washington Post/Contributor/The Washington Post/Getty Images; p. 24 Peter Dean/Shutterstock.com; p. 29 Marc Serota/Stringer/Getty Images Sport/Getty Images.

Printed in the United States of America

CPSIA compliance information: Batch #CS17GS: For further information contact Gareth Stevens, New York, New York at 1-800-542-2595.

CONTENTS

Words in the glossary appear in **bold** type the first time they are used in the text.

THE RIGHT WAY

Lacrosse is a special sport to many people in North America. Though the game is played by many different groups around the world, Native Americans were the first to play a lacrosse-like game called stickball. Over the years, it has changed into what we know as lacrosse today.

There's a lot to learn about lacrosse. For starters, what kind of lacrosse do you play? Did you know the difference between the boys' game and the girls' game? And do you play indoors or outdoors? Knowing the answers to those questions is just the start of knowing your position in this great game.

CENTURIES OLD

Lacrosse was named by early French explorers who first saw native peoples playing stickball. "Crosse" has to do with the curved stick they carried the ball with. Though three different kinds of stickball were played by different native groups, girls' lacrosse today is much more closely related to the kinds of lacrosse played by Native Americans.

LACROSSE IS A FAST AND EXCITING SPORT, ESPECIALLY IF YOU KNOW HOW TO PLAY THE RIGHT WAY.

DIFFERENT KINDS

Boys and girls use slightly different lacrosse **equipment**, and that's because they play a slightly different game. The point of lacrosse is to score goals on the other team's net. But how that happens is different in each game.

LACROSSE FIELDS

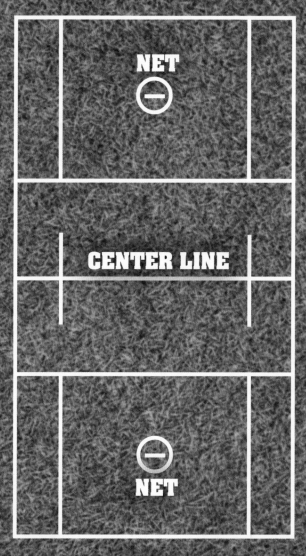

BOYS

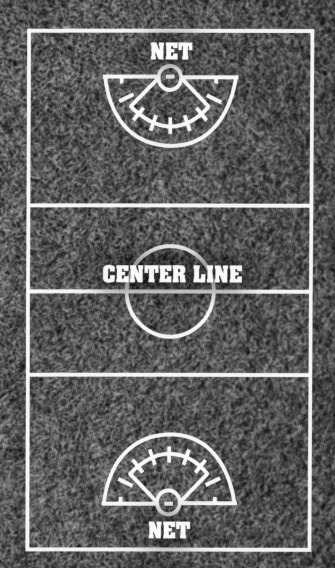

GIRLS

Lacrosse is a game with its own special equipment. But the equipment is different for boys and girls. Girls' lacrosse doesn't allow contact, so they wear less equipment. Girls need a lacrosse stick, eye protection, and a mouth guard to play. Some girls wear special gloves, too.

Boys' lacrosse allows stick and body contact, so players need to wear more pads. They must wear shoulder pads, rib pads, arm pads, and gloves. They also need a special helmet and mouth guard to keep them safe. Goaltenders in both sports wear extra equipment because they have to stop lacrosse balls traveling at high speeds.

STICK WITH IT

Lacrosse sticks are different for boys and girls, too. A girls' lacrosse stick is made of a shaft, or pole, that has a small net on one end for a lacrosse ball to sit in. A boys' lacrosse stick has a deeper net used to cradle, or carry, a ball.

BOYS HAVE TO WEAR MUCH MORE EQUIPMENT THAN GIRLS DO WHEN PLAYING LACROSSE.

Boys' lacrosse has four basic positions. The first is the goaltender. He defends the net by standing in the area just in front of it, called the crease. He needs to have quick **reflexes** to get in front of hard shots from the other team's offense. Goaltenders need to see the field well and follow the ball, even when it's taken into the area behind the net.

Goaltenders have a special lacrosse stick with a much bigger net than other players. They also wear a chest protector to keep them safe from hard shots taken by the other team.

TALK ABOUT IT!

Goaltenders need to talk to their teammates! This helps the group defend the net together. A goalie needs to help his defenders stay in front of the other team's attack and make sure other players don't get open for free shots. They also can start a team's offense with a good pass if they stop a shot and get possession of the ball!

A HARD LACROSSE BALL CAN HURT IF A GOALTENDER DOESN'T USE HIS PADS TO STOP A SHOT. OUCH!

STAYING BEHIND

Defenders in boys' lacrosse work hard to stop their **opponent's** offense from scoring goals. It's **tough** to keep up with an offense, but it's an important job. The three players on defense need to have fast feet to keep up with attacking players.

They need to know how to slide over to get in front of players that get passed the ball. Getting in front of them can stop shots on net. They also need to watch for players cutting toward the net looking for passes. Some defenders will use a longer stick on defense. This helps them better defend and intercept, or catch, passes.

STAY ON YOUR SIDE

Defenders need to stay in their own end during play. Even if the ball goes to a team's offensive end, the three defenders can't follow their teammates onto that side of the field. They have to stay back with the goaltender and watch what happens. They make sure they're ready for play to come back, though!

LONG-STICK DEFENSEMEN MAY LOOK STRANGE, BUT THEY PLAY AN IMPORTANT ROLE ON A LACROSSE TEAM. THEY USE THAT LONG STICK TO GET IN THE OFFENSE'S WAY!

ALL OVER THE FIELD

Midfielders have many different jobs. These three players can move all over the field, helping the defense to stop the other team from scoring and setting up the attackers with good passes to score goals. While midfielders don't score very often, they can take shots on net and need to be smart to know where to be on the field at all times.

Some midfielders also use long sticks like defensemen. They help a team transition, or move from defense to offense and back again. A great midfielder can help on both sides of the game, playing tough defense and helping his team score in a matter of seconds!

Being able to read the play, or see where the ball is going and what the other team is doing, is a huge part of a midfielder's job. Making a long pass to an attacker when the opponent's midfielders are out of position, for example, can lead to a chance for their team to score!

HERE'S THE BASIC SETUP OF A BOYS' LACROSSE TEAM.

BOYS' FIELD POSITIONS

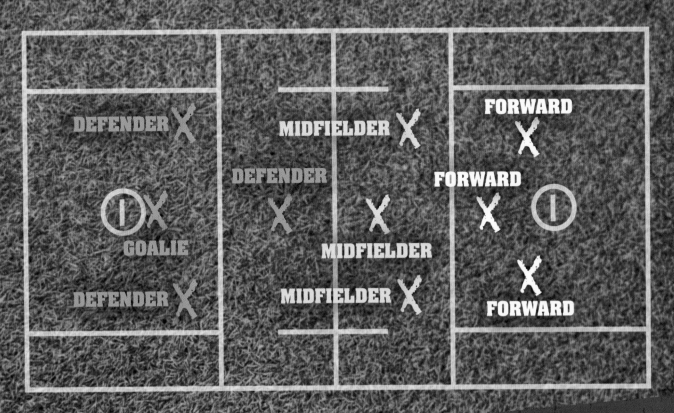

DEFENDER X

MIDFIELDER X

FORWARD X

DEFENDER

FORWARD

GOALIE

X

X

FORWARD

X

MIDFIELDER

DEFENDER X

MIDFIELDER X

X

FORWARD

Forwards, or attackers, get all the attention in lacrosse. They stay on the attacking side of the field at all times and try to score goals. These players are fast and can shoot at the net with great **accuracy**. They must also be tough, as the other team's defense will try to knock them down and take away the ball.

Making accurate passes is also important in lacrosse. So is getting away from the other team's defenders. Attacking players often cross paths to mix up defenders and get open for chances to score. This is called setting a pick!

TRACK IT DOWN!

In field lacrosse, the ball often goes out of play behind the goaltender. But unlike basketball or other sports, the team that sent the ball out doesn't lose possession. Instead, the team that has a player closest to the ball when it went out of play gets it. That means a lot of chasing for attacking players!

MORE OPTIONS

Because girls' lacrosse doesn't allow contact, the game is more about speed and **agility** on offense and how defenders try to stop it. Girls' lacrosse has the same four basic positions—goaltender, defender, midfielder, and attacker. But with two more players on each team, there are different, more specialized ways the players in these positions play.

Many of the boys' lacrosse rules also apply in girls' lacrosse. Four attackers must stay in the offensive half of the field at all times, and five defenders—including the goalie—must stay in the defensive end.

DIFFERENT MARKINGS

Girls' lacrosse has more players and also a different field setup. Most fields are 120 yards (109 m) long and 60 yards (54.8 m) wide. Rather than one line at midfield, there are **restraining lines** 30 yards (27 m) from each goal that attackers or defenders cannot cross. The crease is also different in girls' lacrosse—it spreads out like a fan.

THIS IS HOW A GIRLS' LACROSSE TEAM LINES UP ON THE FIELD. COMPARED TO BOYS' LACROSSE, THE TWO EXTRA POSITIONS ARE USUALLY FILLED BY AN ADDITIONAL DEFENDER AND ATTACKER.

GIRLS' FIELD POSITIONS

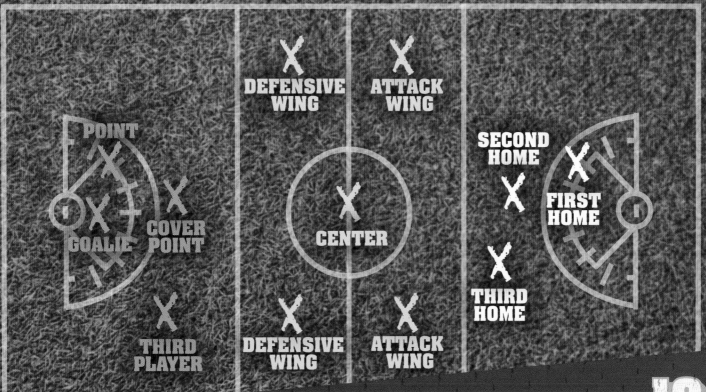

POINT

COVER POINT

GOALIE

THIRD PLAYER

DEFENSIVE WING

ATTACK WING

CENTER

DEFENSIVE WING

ATTACK WING

SECOND HOME

FIRST HOME

THIRD HOME

The most important defender in girls' lacrosse is the point. This player works with the goaltender to organize the defense in front of the net. She tells other defenders where to go and whom to cover on the field. The point stays close to the net, trying to take away passes for the opposing offense.

Cover point is another important defensive position. She needs good footwork to stay with an offensive player, called the second home, who will try to score goals. The cover point also works in transition, taking a pass from the goalie and passing the ball up to attackers.

ON THIRD

Another defensive position is called the third player. The third player's job is to keep tabs on the opponent's offensive player called the third home. She needs to have good reflexes to keep track of this speedy player. Third players also need to read the other team's offense to take away passing lanes and break up plays before an offense can shoot.

LEFT, RIGHT, AND CENTER

The middle of the field in girls' lacrosse often has five players in it. The most important one is the center. She takes face-offs and helps both the offense and defense get set up. Centers are often the team's best player! They can play all over the field and have many different skills that make them good on offense and defense.

The left and right defensive wings, or outside wings, stay on the sides of the center circle near the sidelines. These wings defend the attack wings of the other team. Defensive wings need to be good at running a long way!

FACE-OFF!

Face-offs, or the move that starts play, are different in girls' and boys' lacrosse. The centers in girls' lacrosse put their sticks together, and an official puts the ball between them. When the whistle blows, they raise and pull back their sticks and try to get possession of the ball. In boys' lacrosse, two players fight for the ball on the ground!

ATTACKING WINGS AND HOMES

Midfielders often play big roles on offense in girls' lacrosse. The left and right attack wings, for example, help the offense get set up in the attacking zone. Wingers play on the outside edges of the field and help the home players score goals. They may not score many goals, but are often responsible for helping make them happen.

One of three main attack positions, the third home, is often the player who's the best passer. Third homes set up the offense by feeding passes to the attack wings as well as second and first home. They sometimes take shots on net, but are best at getting assists.

GET BACK!

Midfielders like the center and left and right defensive wings need to be smart because they play all over the field. Getting back on defense can help stop an opponent's attack and start your own! Knowing what the other team is trying to do on offense can help not only stop them, but also control the game and help your offense score goals.

EVERYONE NEEDS TO KNOW HOW TO SHOOT, BUT PASSING IS OFTEN MORE IMPORTANT IN LACROSSE. GOOD PASSES MAKE GOOD GOALS!

The two most important attacking positions are second home and first home. Second home often runs the offense in girls' lacrosse, like a point guard in basketball. They tell attackers what play to run or where to go to set up a scoring chance. Being able to handle the ball well is a great skill for a second home, as she often has the ball on offense.

The first home's job is to get shots off and score goals. She must be fast and able to get away from defenders. First homes are the most offensive-minded players on the field.

PENALTIES

When a player does something wrong in lacrosse, they're called for a penalty. They go off the field for a set period of time, and their team has to play with one less player on the field. This makes it easier for the team not penalized to score goals, so be careful out there!

KEEP GOING

Now that you know the basics of boys' and girls' lacrosse, you can take the field for yourself. But there's so much more to learn. There's a lot of **strategy** in lacrosse, and a good team often has a good coach who can give them good direction on the field.

Lacrosse is a game full of individual skill, but it's important that players learn to play well together. Using your teammates to pass well and set up good scoring chances is how you win. So make sure you play with your friends and learn what they're good at to become a great team!

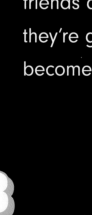

Coaches are an important part of any team. They can help you figure out what position is best for you and teach you more about the things you need to do in that role. Always listen to your coach, who can teach you how to play smart and—most importantly—play safe!

PRACTICE IS WHERE GOOD TEAMS BECOME GREAT. IT CAN BE FUN TO WORK ON YOUR SKILLS!

GLOSSARY

accuracy: the state of being free from mistakes; the ability to hit the target

agility: able to move quickly and easily

equipment: the tools needed for a certain purpose

opponent: the person or team you must beat to win a game

penalty: loss or harm caused because of a broken rule

reflexes: the ability to react quickly

restraining: limiting; keeping back

strategy: a plan of action to achieve a goal

tough: hard; able to keep working and focus on a task

FOR MORE INFORMATION

BOOKS

Bowker, Paul. *Total Lacrosse*. Minneapolis, MN: ABDO Publishing, 2017.

Meister, Cari. *Lacrosse*. Minneapolis, MN: Jump!, 2017.

Rogers, Kate. *Girls Play Lacrosse*. New York, NY: PowerKids Press, 2016.

WEBSITES

The Positions on a Boys' Lacrosse Team
dummies.com/sports/lacrosse/the-positions-on-a-boys-lacrosse-team/
Learn more about lacrosse and how to play the game.

Positions on a Girls' Lacrosse Team
dummies.com/sports/lacrosse/positions-on-a-girls-lacrosse-team/
Find out what's different about girls' lacrosse here.

Rules: Keeping the Game Fair
uslacrosse.org/rules
Learn more about lacrosse and the equipment you need to play
the game.

INDEX